Copyright

Copyright © 2010 by Max Smith

All rights reserved. This book or any portion thereof

may not be reproduced or used in any manner whatsoever

without the express written permission of the publisher

except for the use of brief quotations in a book review.

Study Skills:

How to Prepare for Exams, Term Papers and Essays

Table of Contents

TAKING NOTES 8

READING ASSIGNMENTS 16

MEMORY 26

PLANNING AND ORGANIZATION 34

FOCUS AND CONCENTRATION 43

PROCRASTINATION 51

STUDYING FOR EXAMS 60

TEST ANXIETY 68

PAPERS AND ESSAYS 76

EXERCISE 83

FINAL WORDS 91

How to Make Yourself Study Even When You Have No Motivation

Let's be honest with each other here. You've probably spent more time scrolling through Instagram and Facebook than you have studying in the past few hours. Right?

You probably have some huge assignment that's staring at you from your desk right now, but the thought of doing any work on that assignment right now is the last thing on your mind because you have literally no motivation to do it.

And if you're feeling that way, well you're not alone. I feel that way all the time. And despite all the years I have put into writing books and running my businesses, at least once a week I run into a situation where I have to do something and I have basically no motivation to do it.

So this is a pretty common problem. And despite those immortal words from Shia LaBeouf constantly ringing in our heads ... - Just do it! A lot of us continually deal with it.

Now within the realm of productivity, there are both long term fixes and short term fixes. And for a problem like this, a problem of motivation, long term fixes would be things like building better self-discipline or building strong habits or creating a better study space.

But in this chapter I want to focus on the short term fixes. If you have something that you need to get done today, but you're feeling completely unmotivated, what can you do? Well I'm going to go through a four step process that I go through every single time that I'm feeling this way.

And through personal experience over several years, I have learned that doing these things really does help, even if my brain tells me that, this time I really am having an off day. This time it's not going to work. When I actually take the time and put in the effort to put these things into practice, they really do help.

Go Outside for A Walk

This is probably the simplest practice on the list. But it's also the one that my brain always tries to convince itself that it doesn't need to do. Because when I have a lot of work to do, the thought of getting up from my desk and going outside, seems like a huge waste of time.

But every single time that I do it, when I'm feeling unmotivated or I'm dealing with brain fog, it always helps to raise my motivation levels and clear my head. Now I could tell you all sorts of scientific evidence about why this is true.

For instance, Dr. John Ratey's book, "Spark," goes into all sorts of detail about how exercise raises your cognitive abilities after you do it. And there are also studies that show that Vitamin D, which you get primarily through sunlight exposure, can help with symptoms of fatigue. And there's also the Japanese concept of Shinrin-Yoku, or forest bathing, which asserts that exposure to nature, you know forests and trees like this, can have all sorts of health benefits.

But the main thing I want to share here is my personal experience with this practice. Because my ability to focus is always 100% of the time improved when I choose to go for a walk. Or to be more accurate, whenever I choose to go outside and do any kind of exercise. Could be playing basketball or skateboarding.

The reason I chose to focus on walking here is that it's easy. You don't need any equipment. You don't need a basketball. You don't need a bike. And you can even do it if it's cold. As they say in Norway, there is no such thing as bad weather, only bad clothes.

Focus On One Specific Task

So once you've gone out and finished that walk and you brought your mental energy up just a little bit, the next thing on the list to do is to decide on one specific task to work on.

If you have a to do list with multiple items on it, put it away. You need to commit to a single task and you don't want that to do list to be a temptation to jump to something else once it gets difficult. It's all about committing.

Imagine a hamster ball with three different hamsters in it. If all those hamsters are trying to go their own little separate direction, then that hamster ball is going to go nowhere. But if they all decide to go in one direction, well they're probably going to trip all over each other because hamster balls were not designed for multiple hamsters, but luckily your brain is not a hamster ball.

And when you decide on one specific direction to go in and you commit to it, you make progress. Now you can make this commitment purely mental. But I also find that it sometimes works to pull out a scrap of paper and write down the task that you decide to work on, so that way it can be sitting next to you on your desk and constantly reminding you if you start to forget.

And if you want an electronic solution, there's also a chrome extension called momentum, which basically replaces your new tab screen with a cool wallpaper and it lets you decide on one singular focus that you can type in and then set. Alright onto step three in the process.

Clean Up Your Environment

Once you've decided on that one task you're going to work on, the next step is to clear to neutral. This means to clear up your work space, your desk, and your desktop on your computer, and setting that space back to a state where it's prepped for that single task you decided to work on and nothing else.

Anthony Bourdain talks about a similar concept in his book, "Kitchen Confidential." He talks about how a chef that he used to work with went up to one of his line cooks and ran his hands across the cooks really dirty, crumb-filled cutting board, put it up to his face and said, this is what your brain looks like. Work clean.

When your work area is organized and set up for the task that you have decided on, you are going to work on that task a lot more effectively.

Low Effort Hack

Finally, to actually get yourself into the process of doing the task, utilize what I like to call, the low effort hack. This is a useful little mental hack that I use, on pretty much, a daily basis.

Usually when I feel mental resistance to a task, like researching for a book I'm writing, that mental resistance is usually because of how difficult it is to do the task well.

If I'm writing a book, usually I feel resistance writing the next paragraph because I feel like it needs to have a word play or a funny reference. And when I'm researching, I know that it's going to be difficult to actually find the scientific studies or the quotes or pictures that will back up what I'm trying to say.

But, and this is where the whole low effort thing comes in, what isn't difficult is just writing what's on the top of my mind right now. If I can't come up with a joke or a reference that will make the segment I'm writing funnier, that's fine. I'll just write what's in my head right now and I'll come back and make it funnier later. And it's the exact same story when I'm referencing research.

If I really don't want to go find the exact source or that one fact that I'm trying to reference, then I won't. In the script I'll put in brackets and all caps, reference that one study and figure out where it came from, and then I'll do that later.

Now doing this means that you're creating something that you're going to have to come back and fix later on. But that's okay. Remember the blank page is the enemy. It's far easier to come back and fix an imperfect mess later on, then it is to create something perfect from scratch on the first try.

That imperfect mess gives you hand holds that you can grab onto. Additionally, another huge benefit of starting from a place of low effort, is that sometimes you just need a little bit of a warm up to get yourself into a place where you're really creative and in the zone.

Back when I was a teenager, my dad had a weight training schedule for me and my brother. We had to work out at least three times a week. And sometimes I'd come down into the gym with him and I'd say, dad today is an off day, I really just want to go light. I'm not feeling it. And I will never forget what he told me on one of those occasions. He said that sometimes you hit your PRs, your personal records, on off days. And I'm actually not making this up, this really did happen.

One of those days I came down to the basement, I said dad, it's an off day. So he had me go through a longer than normal warm-up period and on that day, I actually hit a PR. In fact, I think it was actually 225, which if you're a weightlifter you know is two plates on each side of the bar, and that was one of the mentally, most difficult PRs for me to hit. It took me a really long time to get.

So that should serve as an illustration. Even if you feel like today is an off day, just use that low effort hack and put some time in. There is a big difference between your state of mind before you start working and your state of mind once you're in the flow state. Once you're immersed in your project. The trick is just getting yourself there.

Taking Notes

Why focus on your notes? Well, simply put, when it comes to learning and retaining information, output is just as important as input.

When you're first learning a fact or a concept, you're absorbing new information; but, to retain that information for a long time, you need to store it in a place that you can easily access later on, and you need to put it in your own words. Before we talk about specific note-taking systems, what information you should actually record in your notes, and whether or not it's helpful to blend them up and drink them like a milkshake, let's start with what's going to set you up for success in the first place.

Showing Up to Class Prepared with The Right Tools

There are three routes you can go when selecting those tools: paper, computer, or arm. What's the best option? Well, unless you're that guy from Memento, we can probably narrow it down to either paper or computer.

Between those two, there's been a debate going on for years, but we do have some recent scientific evidence that we can turn to for some hard answers.

According to a study done at Princeton University in 2014, students who took notes on a 15-minute lecture using a laptop wrote an average of 310 words, while those who wrote on paper only averaged 173.

So it seems typing your notes definitely does give you a speed advantage. The downside to becoming the metaphorical Speed Racer of note-taking, though, was that these same students were able to recall less information when tested later on. So why does this happen? Well, the root of the problem lies in the fact that the computer note-takers were much more likely to record what was being presented word-for-word. Let's go to the Thought Bubble.

When you're paying attention to a lecture, there are two aspects to the information being presented. Since complex information is communicated through language – be it written or spoken – we get both the syntax (like the letters and sounds that make up the words) as well as the meaning.

When you're typing out your notes, the speed advantage enables you to record a much more complete version of what your teacher is saying. However, your working memory – the part of your memory that deals with the information you're currently absorbing – can only deal with so much at one time.

Current cognitive science research puts that amount at around four "chunks" of information, which we'll talk about in another chapter. The combination of that recording speed advantage and your built-in mental processing limit can lead you to devote more mental resources to the syntax of the message – those pesky letters and sounds – and less to the actual meaning. As a result, you learn less in class and you create more work for yourself later on.

So, does this mean that a pen and paper always beats your laptop? Well, not necessarily. Now that you know that the speed increase you get through typing has a downside, you can just resolve to type less and pay more attention to the meaning of the message while you're in class.

Still, paper does have an implicit advantage, as it requires less self-control. Your long-hand writing speed automatically limits how much you pay attention to the syntax, and – as a bonus – you don't have to worry about being tempted to go on Facebook in the middle of class either.

Regardless of what tool you decide to choose, though, make sure you come into class prepared. If you're using paper, have a well-organized notebook with plenty of blank space, as well as a good quality pen that you enjoy writing with. And if you decide that a computer fits your style better, find a good note-taking app like Evernote, or OneNote, Dropbox Paper, or any other that fits your fancy.

You should also close out of any apps or websites that aren't relevant to the lecture – that'll help you stay focused, though you still might have to work to ignore that guy in front of you who's taking a quiz on Buzzfeed to figure out his Hogwarts house.

What Do I Write Down?

Now that you're prepped and equipped with the right tools, what exactly should you be recording with them? After all, you can't just record everything.

As the famous mathematician Eric Temple Bell noted, "The map is not the thing mapped." Just like a map is only useful if it summarizes and simplifies what it represents, your notes are a useful reviewing tool only when there's a high signal-to-noise ratio. That means they've got to be packed with the information you need to know for tests and later application, and devoid of anything that doesn't matter.

It's a bit hard to make specific recommendations here, since there are so many different subjects and classes in which you'll need your note-taking skills; however, we can put forth some general guidelines that will point you in the right direction.

First and foremost, gauge each class you're taking early on. Carefully look at the syllabus, pay attention to any study guides or review materials you can get your hands on, and make mental notes about different types of questions you see on early quizzes and tests.

Additionally, any time you hear your professor say something like, "This is important, pay attention," in lecture, that's a cue to take extra-careful notes. A lot of my friends in school thought it was a cue to take a nap, but they were wrong.

Beyond that, whether you're sitting in class or going through a reading assignment in your textbook, you'll want to pay special attention to things like:

- Summaries
- Overviews
- Conclusions
- Bullet Lists (Like this one)
- Terms and Definitions
- Examples

Examples are doubly important, especially in classes where you have to apply concepts and formulas to problems, like in math or physics. You can probably remember times when an example presented in class made perfect sense, but then a later homework problem using the same exact concept completely stumped you.

There's a big difference between being able to follow along while someone else solves a problem and having the chops to solve it on your own. But by recording every detail of the examples you see in class – as well as making side notes about why the concepts being used work – you'll have a lot more ammunition to work with while you're tackling those homework problems.

Now that we've covered the elements of good, useful notes, let's get into the specifics of how to take them. There are plenty of note-taking systems out there, each with their own pros and cons, but we're just going to focus on three: The Outline method, the Cornell method, and the Mind-Mapping method.

The Outline Method

This is probably the simplest one of them all, and it's likely the one you're most familiar with. To use it, you just record the details of the lecture or book you're reading in a bullet list. Each main point will be a top-level bullet, and underneath it you'll indent further and further as you add details and specifics.

The Outline method is great for creating well-organized notes, but because it's so rigid, you can easily end up with a ton of notes that all look the same. So to prevent that from happening, use formatting tricks to make important details stand out when you're reviewing them later on. For example, you can make an important note bold to make it stand out.

The Cornell Method

Developed by the Cornell University professor Walter Pauk back in the 1950's and popularized in his book How to Study in College, the Cornell method is a time-tested system that involves dividing your paper (or a table in your note-taking app) into three distinct sections: **The Cue Column**, **The Notes Column**, and **The Summary Column**.

During a lecture, take your actual notes in the aptly-named Notes Column. Here you can use any method you want, be it the standard outline method we just talked about or something more flexible.

At the same time, when you think of questions that weren't answered – or that would be great prompts for later review – write them down in the Cue Column. These questions will come in handy when you're going through your notes in the future, as they'll point you to the most important information and help to frame your thinking.

The Summary Area will remain empty until the lecture is over. Once that time comes, take two or three minutes to briefly look over the notes you took and the questions you wrote down, and then write a 1-2 sentence summary of the biggest ideas that were covered. This serves as an initial review, which helps to consolidate everything that was presented up here and to solidify your understanding while everything is still fresh in your mind.

If neither of these two methods seems like the right fit for you, you might like the final method we're going to cover.

Mind Mapping

Mind maps are diagrams that visually represent the relationships between individual concepts and facts. Like outline-style maps, they're very hierarchical – but that's where the similarities end. Outline-style notes are linear and read much like normal text, while mind maps look more like trees or spider webs.

To create a mind map, you write the main concept smack-dab in the middle of the page, and then branch out from there to flesh out the details. This method works really well on paper, but there are also apps like Coggle which will let you create mind maps on your computer as well.

So what's the best method? Well, that's up for you to decide. I recommend trying each one out, and making your own tweaks as you go along. Also, remember that not every class will work best with the exact same method. Your history notes are probably going to look pretty different from your math notes.

Reading Assignments

You know that little voice in the back of your head that's telling you it's impossible to read all 847 pages your teacher assigned you last week? It's right. To counter that with some good news, though: that's ok!

In this chapter we're going to be diving deep into how you can make the most out of the time you spend on reading assignments, both by learning how to boost your reading speed and how to remember more of what you read.

Do I Actually Need to Read?

First, I want to jump right in and ask the same question that you probably ask yourself every time you look at a syllabus: "Do I actually need to do all this reading?". While some of your teachers might object, the answer is no, and that's because your time isn't limitless.

In a perfect world, you'd be able to pour over every detail of every book in the world and become smarter than Jimmy Neutron. But in this world, you've got other things competing for space in your schedule, like homework, socialising, and tons more. There are other reasons, as well – like, sometimes you'll see a lot of overlap between what's in the book and what you'll hear in lectures.

So, how do you know what reading to actually do? Cal Newport's book How to Become a Straight-A Student provides a pretty good framework for answering that question. He divides assigned readings into two groups; assignments from the class's favored source, which is usually the main textbook, and supplemental readings. You should generally do all the readings from each favored source, but you can afford to be a bit more selective when it comes to the supplemental readings.

Cal provides a hierarchy for prioritizing them, where readings that make an argument take precedence over descriptions of events or people, which in turn are more important than anything that provides context – like press clippings or speeches. What I'll add to that, though, is that every class is different.

Sometimes you'll find that everything in the textbook is mirrored in the lecture slides, and other times you'll still need to look through the reading assignments, but skimming for important main concepts and vocab terms will suffice. And, of course, some classes will require you to barricade yourself in your room with 6 week's rations and those freaky eye things from A Clockwork Orange to hold your eyes open.

But by carefully paying attention and gauging each one, you'll be able to make smart decisions about what to read, skim, or skip.

Speed Reading

Aside from doing some triage on your reading assignments, the other main way to get through them faster is to learn how to read more quickly. We have to be careful here, though, because this is where the term "speed reading" starts getting thrown around and you get people claiming they can teach you to read 1000 words per minute or more.

Sadly, that just isn't possible. As much as I'd love to be able to plow through an entire book over my morning coffee, we humans have some hard-wired limits on how far we can push our reading speeds.

Your visual range is made up of three areas, the fovea, parafovea, and periphery. Of these, only the fovea has a high enough density of cones, the type of photoreceptor cell in your eye that can perceive small details, to make out text on a page.

Since the fovea is pretty small, your eyes read text by making quick jerky movements called saccades. In between each of these saccades is a small pause called a fixation, and this is when the eye intakes the 1-2 words it's currently focused on and sends them to your prefrontal cortex for processing.

Both saccades and fixations take time to do, which essentially sets a speed limit on how fast you can visually process text. And that's just for recognizing the actual letters and words; there are other factors that contribute to a lower speed limit for how quickly you can read text and comprehend it.

The main one is your working memory constraints. Just like the RAM in a computer, your working memory can only process so much at once. Right now, cognitive science quantifies that at about 4-7 bits or "chunks" of information, which we'll talk about more in the next chapter on how your memory works. For now, it's enough to say that you need to give your working memory time to deal with each chunk that comes in before feeding it another one, and you do this by pausing frequently while you're reading.

Additionally, even skilled readers spend about 15% of their reading on regressions, in which the eye moves backwards to re-read text. That time is split between small regressions due to saccades that went too far the first time, and larger ones that are needed for comprehension.

Now, your speed is helped by the fact that you naturally skip words when reading, and your brain is incredibly good at knowing which ones to skip while still retaining good comprehension. Studies have shown that while reading, your eyes fixate on about 85% of the content words – the words that carry the actual ideas – and only about 35% of the function words, which are the "glue" words like "the, and, if," etc.

But even with the speed boost that comes from this intelligent word skipping, research has shown that skilled, college-level readers can expect to read from anywhere between 200-400 words per minute.

For the vast majority of us, anything beyond 400 is getting into skimming territory, where your comprehension starts dropping really quick. "But what about speed reading techniques?" you might ask.

The people that run those speed reading seminars and claim they can read at 2,000 words per minute say that there are techniques out there for breaking past that normal speed range. Like increasing the amount of text you process during each fixation, flashing words in one spot rapidly, and eliminating "subvocalization" – that voice that reads "aloud" in your head when you read silently. Sadly, each of these techniques has been tested scientifically and shown to be ineffective.

For one, increasing the size of each fixation through "training" would be pretty tough, since you would literally have to grow more cones in your eyes. And if you figure out how to do that, I recommend not telling anyone unless they say they're from the X-men.

Additionally, this idea still wouldn't do anything about your working memory constraints, which is the main problem that also plagues Rapid Serial Visual Processing, or RSVP, a technique that involves flashing words rapidly in one spot. The idea here is to eliminate the need for saccades, but it breaks down because it doesn't allow the brain to intelligently skip function words or to do any regressions. This has the dual effect of overtaxing your working memory and not allowing you to go back over a line you didn't understand the first time.

And finally, eliminating subvocalization is a misguided idea because that inner voice is actually quite important. As the researcher Elizabeth Schotter noted: "Attempts to eliminate inner speech have been shown to result in impairments in comprehension when texts are reasonably difficult and require readers to make inferences."

At this point it might seem like I'm the bad guy, and that your only hope is to get on Amazon and buy those Clockwork Orange eye things, but there is hope. Like any other skill, you can become better at reading. The main way to do this is to simply practice. Read often, read widely, and make sure the material is suitably difficult.

Those dense chapters in your psychology textbook aren't going to get any easier if you practice on One Fish, Two Fish, Red Fish, Blue Fish – though that is a great book.

Day-Dreaming

Another problem that might bring down your reading speed is daydreaming.

When I'm reading, I'll sometimes get lost thinking about a specific sentence and end up staring into space, which wastes a ton of time and makes the other people around me wonder if I'm dead. If you have this problem as well, you can set a time goal for the chapter; when I do this, I don't always finish on time, but it does help me stay focused.

Skimming

Finally, when you're reading books that don't require you to comprehend every word, you can speed things up with the pseudo-skimming technique. Skim the text while keeping an eye out for main ideas, vocabulary terms, and anything else important.

When you notice one, slow down and read the entire paragraph that encompasses it. A good way to spot these is to pay special attention to the first and last sentence of each paragraph, as well as any bolding, italics, or other formatting. Looking out for those little bits of formatting will also help you to remember what you read, which is what we're going to shift our focus to now.

Highlighting

One of the most common ways that students attempt to remember what they read is through highlighting – which, to be fair, is useful if done right. The problem is that it's really easy to highlight too much since everything seems important when you're first reading it. And this works against you because it's easy to believe that you "know" the things you've highlighted. When you look back through your book later on, you'll see them, think, "Oh yeah, I remember highlighting that!" and you might decide that you've memorized it. But there are two ways to remember something: You can recall it, or you can recognize it.

The danger with highlighting is that it becomes very easy to mistake recognition – which requires a cue – with true recall, which involves pulling the memory from the depths of your brain's archives all on your own. The more you highlight, the greater this danger becomes.

So if you do decide to highlight your book, be very selective about what gets highlighted. A better idea might be to adopt what Cal Newport calls the Morse Code Method. Here's how he explains it:

First, if you come across a sentence that seems to be laying out a big, interesting idea, draw a quick dot next to it in the margin of the book. Secondly, if you come across an example or explanation that supports the previous big idea, draw a quick dash next to it in the margin. This lets you avoid slowing down while reading, which enables you to smoothly move through and comprehend the whole text before going back to review. Once you do, the dots and dashes will allow you to take smarter notes on what you've read.

Active Reading

Speaking of notes, it's finally time to talk about active reading. This is the process of truly engaging with the text instead of passively just running your eyes over it, which will help you retain a lot more of what you read.

Lots of study books and teachers explain active reading in terms of a system called SQ3R, which stands for Survey, Question, Read, Recite, and Review. Surveying is essentially pre-reading.

Before you start an assignment, skim over the whole thing quickly. Look over the beginning overview, the headings, and any review questions at the end of the chapter. Doing this primes your brain in advance, which will help the most important information stick out later.

You can actually see how well priming works right now. Close your eyes for a few seconds and concentrate on a specific color. When you open them, you'll easily notice that color in the environment around you. Surveying does the same thing with text.

Questioning simply involves writing out some questions that come to mind before starting the reading. I actually do this quite often before researching my book topics, as it helps to – again – prime my brain to pick out the important bits and not spend too much time off in the weeds.

Reading...well, that's reading. That leads into reciting, which is a catch-all word for either taking notes or summarizing what you've read. Now, if you had infinite time, you could do both, but since you probably don't, I'll note that summaries will be more useful for big concepts you need to understand intimately, and more detailed notes will be better for fact-heavy readings.

I don't think you need to follow SQ3R perfectly in order to get the benefits of active reading. In fact, I don't recommend many rigid, acronym-based systems at all. Except for, maybe, SCAR: Stop Complaining and Read.

Memory

In this chapter we're digging into how your memory works and how you can make it work better.

The science of how memory works is complicated, to say the least. After all, how do we explain how a bunch of nerve cells, chemicals, and electrical jolts somehow let you remember algebra, where you left your car keys, important dates, names? Well, it's simple.

Understanding how your memory works will help you to optimize the way you study. Your brain turns information into memories by putting it through a few different stages.

The first is sensory memory, which processes pretty much everything your senses detect or experience in the real world. That sensory memory has the attention span of a five-year-old at the DMV, though, so most of what it takes in is lost almost immediately.

But what does stick moves into your short-term or working memory. This type of memory is sort of like the RAM in your computer – the memories don't stick around permanently. In fact, unless you continuously rehearse what's floating around in working memory, it'll pull a disappearing act after about 15-30 seconds. This can also happen if you try to cram too much in at once, because your working memory can really only handle 4-7 bits or items of information at a time.

Now you can somewhat increase this limit by grouping bits into chunks – like splitting "FBIKGBCIA" into FBI, KGB, CIA, but there's still a limit.

Now, all this happens primarily in your brain's prefrontal cortex, but eventually the information has to make its way to other areas of the brain if it's going to be encoded in long-term memory. The whole process of memory formation causes physical changes within your brain: neurotransmitters shuttle all over the place, neural pathways are forged, and neurons themselves undergo structural improvements using proteins such as brain-derived neurotrophic factor, or BDNF.

And, just like the process of strengthening your muscles through exercise, this all takes time – which is why cramming for a test doesn't work, and why you can't instantly just download jujitsu into your brain like Neo.

As Pierce J. Howard noted in his book The Owner's Manual for the Brain: "Work involving higher mental functions, such as analysis and synthesis, needs to be spaced out to allow new neural connections to solidify. New learning drives out old learning when insufficient time intervenes."

Now that you have a bit of an understanding of how your memory works, one crucial tip should be clear: you have to space your learning out over time. But we're not going to just leave it at that, because – as cognitive scientists have known for a long time – the way you do that spacing matters quite a bit.

To explain this, let's start with why we forget things in the first place. Part of the reason is that your brain doesn't encode all memories equally. During the long-term encoding process, the hippocampus will use different levels of neurotransmitters based on, among other things, how important the information is. And this plays a big role in how strongly it's embedded in long-term memory.

This filtering mechanism is great for survival, as it allows your brain to safely disregard unimportant things, like what you had for breakfast two weeks ago, while paying special attention to what's important, like that fact that there are ninjas behind you right now.

Unfortunately, you can't always consciously decide what's important and what's not, which is why it can be hard to remember all the details from that history chapter you just read. At a primal level, your brain just doesn't think the details of Genghis Khan's war with the Quarismian Shah in 1219 are as important as a bear attacking you. However, there are a few tricks you can pull to make it care a bit more.

First, understand that your brain latches more readily onto things that are tangible, visual, and uncommon than it does with the abstract or the mundane. Because of this, it can be helpful to develop mnemonics, which are mental devices that help you associate pieces of information in ways that are easier to remember. And mnemonics can take many forms.

You can create sayings to remember sequences of letters – such as "Ernie Ate Dynamite, GoodBye Ernie" to remember the names of the strings on a guitar. Or you can make up weird stories in your head that includes cues to the information you're trying to associate. Like, the way I remember that Helsinki is the capital of Finland is by imagining a giant flaming sinkhole in the ground opening up with a bunch of sharks jumping out of it. Since it's weird, it's easy to remember, and it helps me associate the words Hell, Fin, and Sink, which in turn connect Finland and Helsinki.

Additionally, the more connections that lead to a memory, the stronger it'll be – especially if they're learned in different contexts.

When I first learned about caravels, which were those small ships that Portuguese explorers used to travel down the African coast in the 15th century, I had a hard time remembering that name – caravels. But once I started using them in Civilization V to build my empire – and to make sure Ghandi never got far enough to nuke me, the memory became a lot more solid, since I was interacting with it in a new context.

Of course, you still have to repeatedly access your new memories once they're encoded if you want them to stick around. This is pretty much the iron law of memorization: Except in cases where they're attached to a particularly intense emotional experience, memories fade away unless you repeatedly recall them. Well, sort of.

In the 1880's, a German psychologist named Herman Ebbinghaus wanted to understand how memories decayed over time, and he especially wanted to know how long the process took. He began by running countless tests on his own memory, forcing himself to recall long lists of meaningless letters until eventually, he came up with the Forgetting Curve.

While largely hypothetical and simplistic in its details, this model demonstrated how memories decay quickly unless accessed again and again. Since Ebbinghaus's days, our understanding of how memory decays has come a long way. According to the Forget-to-Learn theory, which is presented in Benedict Carey's book How We Learn, memories actually have two different strengths: storage strength and retrieval strength.

Picture your brain as a library where none of the books ever get stolen or damaged. When a new book is put on a shelf, it's there for good. This represents storage strength, which, according to the theory, doesn't weaken. Once a memory is encoded, the neural pattern can only get stronger.

Now, unfortunately this library has a particularly lazy librarian who doesn't do a very good job of keeping the library's catalog organized. This represents retrieval strength, which does fade with time. Unless you go in and organize the catalog – or recall the memory – you'll eventually lose track of it.

Here's where it gets good. The more a memory's retrieval strength has faded, and the greater the difficulty of recalling it, the greater the increase in learning will be. This is called the Spacing Effect. It's essentially the "No pain, no gain," of the mental realm; the harder you have to work to recall something, the greater the reward for doing so.

There's an obvious catch, though – if you wait too long, the retrieval strength diminishes so much that you won't be able to recall the memory at all. This where the Principle of Desirable Difficulty comes in.

To maximize the efficiency of your studying, you want to the find the point right before you're about to forget something. And you can do this by using spaced repetition techniques. The general idea behind spaced repetition is to steadily increase the amount of time in between each study session for any piece of information. So instead of reviewing a fact or concept once every few days, you'd use a schedule like this where you'd wait a day between the first and second sessions, three days between the second and third, and so on.

To do this precisely, you need a system that tracks your progress in memorizing each piece of information you need to study – since it never happens evenly. If you've got 100 Japanese kanji to learn, it's inevitable that you'll remember some easier than others. If you use the exact same time delays for every kanji, you'll spend too much time studying some, and others won't ever be learned at all.

To solve this problem, you can use the Leitner System. In it, you've got five boxes, each of which represents a specific study interval. Box 1 gets studied every day, Box 2 every three days, Box 3 once a week, and so on. Every fact or term gets its own flash card, and all cards start off in Box 1. Once you get a card right, move it to the next box.

And if you get a card wrong – no matter what box it's in – send it back to Box 1.

If you play by these rules, you'll ensure that you maximize your efficiency by spending more time studying the cards you have the weakest grasp on.

The increasing time intervals of the boxes also help you leverage the spacing effect and get to close to that point of desirable difficulty. There are also a ton of spaced repetition apps for both computers and smartphones that will let you make this whole process digital. The best known one is probably Anki, which is free on most platforms, but there's also TinyCards, Quizlet, and many, many others.

Now when it comes to subjects that aren't easily studied through flash cards – like math or even a sport like skateboarding – it's harder to use a rigid spaced repetition algorithm. However, the spacing effect applies here as well, so be sure to space out your practice over time. During any given day's practice, you'll eventually hit a wall where you stop making progress whether it's learning derivatives in calculus or kick flips in skateboarding – but if you come back to it a few days later, everything will be more likely to click into place.

In each of these study sessions, make sure you're putting the focus on recalling information from your own memory. As we talked about in our video on reading assignments, there are two main kinds of memory – recognition and recall.

Recognition is what happens when you're exposed to information you've already seen before and remember it. But recall involves dredging the information up from the depths of your memory banks without seeing it, which is exactly what you'll have to do in both your exams and in many real-world situations.

So when you study, make sure you're focusing on active recall. Don't just passively read over your notes or slides — use them to create quizzes for yourself, or challenge yourself to sit down and write out a summary of what you've learned from memory.

If you're studying a subject like math or physics, put a huge emphasis on practicing with real problems and actually use the concepts and formulas you've learned. In short, studying should feel like work, and it should challenge your brain. When it does, you'll remember more while spending fewer hours at your desk.

Planning and Organization

As a student, you have two modes, which I like to call Planning Mode and Robot Mode. When you buckle down to study for a test, finish a homework assignment, or slog your way through a textbook chapter, you're in Robot Mode. You're doing the work. But robots can only do what they're programmed to do, and they need a well-maintained environment to work in.

I've seen videos of those robots in car factories – they're not working with dirty laundry or cheeseburger wrappers laying around. Those places are pretty clean. So, if you want your Robot mode to work efficiently, you need to know how to program it and how to create a good environment for it to work in.

Organizational System

To get started, you're going to need an organizational system. This is the framework for storing all information and resources that we'll need, and also for capturing "ideas." An "Idea" is my term for any intangible information that you need to save and have easy access to later on. This can include: Tasks, Events, and actual, you know, ideas – things you want to write, create – anything like that.

Additionally, you'll need a reliable way to store: Notes, Handouts, and any other output you create, be it writing, code, art, or cheeseburger wrapper origami. So let's create that system.

In my mind, any good organizational system worth its salt includes: A task manager, a calendar, a note-taking system and some kind of physical storage for paper documents.

Your task manager is the place where you record the stuff that you need to get done. It's what you look to when you get that sudden burst of motivation to do ALL THE THINGS, and then wonder what all the things actually includes.

You'll find a zillion different types of task managers out there, but there are only a few really essential features. Pick a system that makes it easy to record a task's details and due date, and also make sure it's a snap to see what's coming due in the near future. The task manager that I personally use these days is called Todoist, and it ticks all those boxes. But there are lots of other options, including Trello, Microsoft To-Do, and Any.Do.

And if paper systems are more your speed, the classic day planner works just as well, as do more recent systems like the Bullet Journal method.

In addition to tasks, you'll also need to remember upcoming events, and that's what your calendar is for. Now if you're using an old-fashioned paper planner, then your task manager and calendar might be one in the same – but personally, I've always found that keeping the two separate works better for me. A calendar – in my case, Google Calendar, but it might be Apple's Calendar app or something else for you – is best for events that will happen at a specific time, while a task manager better handles things that have due dates, but that you can work on whenever you want before then.

Next, you need to figure out how to organize your notes. This is pretty simple for paper notes; you just use paper notebooks, and have a separate section or entire notebook for each class. But, for digital notes, you've got a lot of options.

Now, my app of choice has always been Evernote, but you can also take a look at Microsoft's OneNote, Apple's Notes or even Google Docs.

Lastly, make sure you've got some kind of physical storage for handouts, loose papers, and notebooks you've filled up. Keeping one of those portable accordion folders in your bag works well when you're away from home, and it combos well with a file box for longer-term storage.

Once you've cobbled your system together, the next step is to develop an scheme for keeping it all organized. Now, sometimes a scheme is a plan for getting a bunch of small, yellow minions and attempting to steal the moon, and I definitely don't want to discourage you from doing that. But, in this context, it just means a set of rules and conventions that help to keep your system organized and useful.

If you choose a good scheme and stick to its rules every time you file away a new task, event, or handout, then the system will remain useful and you won't find yourself digging through your laundry basket at 3 a.m. looking for that essay you wrote on Hamlet.

Organising Your Desktop

Your computer's file structure is a great place to start, since so many people seem content to just let everything sit out on their desktop. This is a pretty bad scheme to use, because you're eventually going to lose something.

So a better long-term solution is to create a folder structure that's well-defined, yet flexible. My recommendation is to set up your computer's folders like a tree with lots of branches. The top-level folder is the root of the tree, and that's where the scheme starts.

So, in this case, that folder will be called "College." From there, try to create branches that represent the different aspects of that part of your life. The first logical branch point in this situation is the year – freshman, sophomore, junior, senior. Then, as we go further and hit even more specific branch points, choose a logical category for drilling down to the next level.

And this changes depending on the type of information you're organizing. You can even organise by class such as Sports Psychology, History of Rome, and Film Studies 101.

And finally, add subfolders for big group projects. If you're constantly vigilant about saving your work in the correct folder, then this structure will ensure that it's always easy to find what you're looking for – you just go down the branches that lead to it.

You can use a similar structure with your digital notes as well. This is why I like using Evernote so much. Since everything is organized into Notebooks, and Notebooks themselves can be put into stacks, I can create a scheme that organizes my entire life.

For instance, I've got a notebook stack for classes. Within it, every class I've ever taken gets its own notebook, and within those notebooks I can create notes for individual lectures, reading assignments, and other things.

With your calendar, color-code events so you can see which part of your life they represent, like classes, extracurricular activities, and part-time job hours. If you use a paper planner, you can do this by using colored stickers or markers, as well.

Lastly, create projects within your task manager for grouping similar tasks together. If you're a student, the most logical way to do this is to create a project for each class, as well as additional projects for anything else you've got going on.

Now What?

Now that you've chosen your tools and have your system set up, you need to make sure you'll actually use it, since putting things into your system properly takes work. If your teacher assigns something in class, you eventually need to open your task manager and record all the details correctly. That takes more effort than simply tossing that handout into your backpack or telling yourself, "Eh, I'm sure I'll remember it."

But if you don't do it, your system started to get unorganized and incomplete – which means your brain can't rely on it anymore. So you need to build the habit of using your system correctly all the time, even though it takes effort.

One of the best ways to do that is to remove as much friction as you possibly can from the process. This is an idea that I like to call quick capture – figuring out the quickest, easiest way to file things into your system without compromising its structure. There are two main ways to go about practicing quick capture.

The first is to commit to entering things into the correct place the moment they come up. For instance, if your teacher assigns homework in class, you'd immediately open your task manager and record all the details. If you do choose to go this route, you can streamline things by choosing apps and tools that simplify the recording process.

A good example is Google Calendar's iPhone app, which lets you set the date, time, and location of an event just by typing them into the event's title. That's a lot quicker than tapping on each individual field. It also means eliminating any unnecessary features from your system; while it might be cool that your to-do app can add priority levels to each task, you probably don't need them, and they just add more friction to the process.

The second option here is to use a daily note, which is a simple piece of notebook paper, or a note that's quickly accessible on your phone, where you record everything that comes up during the day. This is a temporary holding place. At the end of each day, you need to move everything you've recorded to the correct place within your system.

Weekly vs Daily Planning

All right, so now we are ready to finally dig into the details of planning. Now, I like to view planning in two separate contexts: weekly and daily.

The main purpose of your weekly planning session is to look at everything that's coming due during the upcoming week, as well as in the following one. I recommend doing this on Sunday; that way, you'll be aware of everything that's coming up, and you'll have a rough idea of when you'll be able to work on it all based on what's already in your calendar. However, there is also some long-term planning that should be done here.

First, if you've got an exam coming up in the next month, it's a good idea to look over everything that will be covered, and then to schedule study sessions over the upcoming weeks to ensure you don't find yourself cramming right before it.

If you've just been assigned a big project, you can similarly break that project down into small chunks and assign due dates to those chunks. Think about other big events that might be coming up in your life as well. Maybe there's a scholarship deadline coming up, or a birthday you want to remember. If something comes to mind, add it to your system so you won't forget it.

In addition to planning out your week, you should also take a few minutes each day to create a daily plan. This is simply a list of the events you've got planned and the tasks you want to accomplish. Now you can do this in the morning before you start school, or you can do it at night before you go to bed, which is what I prefer to do. As you create it, try to batch your tasks.

If you have a bunch of easy, low-energy tasks, or errands that require travel, plan ahead and combine them into one big maintenance session. Doing this will help you get them all done in a short, compact block of time, which in turn frees up lots of uninterrupted time that you can dedicate to your really challenging work.

Review Session

Finally, to keep your system running smoothly, choose one day per week to do a review session. And if you want to be extra-efficient, you can just combine it with your weekly planning in order to get it all done in one fell swoop. During this review session, you'll do a couple things.

First, look over your plans and reflect on the past week. Compare what you planned to do with what actually got done, and if there's a gap between the two, try to figure out what caused it. Doing this can help you to pinpoint things that are hurting your productivity – maybe you were distracted a lot, or maybe you simply planned to do too much.

After that, go through your task manager and calendar. If there are any tasks or events that need changes, make them. This prevents what I like to call "entropy" which is a term in thermodynamics that generally refers to how everything in the universe tends to move toward disorder and chaos.

This is exactly what organizational systems tend to do as well, but by regularly bringing them back to order on a weekly basis, you can keep things from getting too chaotic. So now that you've got your system build and your planning habits in place, you're well equipped to tackle all the work your classes are going to throw at you in the most effective way possible.

Additionally, you can rest assured knowing that nothing will slip your mind or fall through the cracks, as long as you keep those habits up.

Focus and Concentration

I want you to ask yourself: when's the last time you were able to sit down and intensely pay attention to one task for a long time? If you're anything like me, this has become harder and harder to do as we've added more distractions to our lives – tweets, snaps, messages, browser tabs, cookies that must be clicked – they're in endless supply, while your brain's ability to resist them is, sadly, not. So that's why in this chapter we're turning our attention to attention itself.

Before we get into any specific tips, let's first answer the question of what attention really is. Put simply, attention is the process of focusing your cognitive resources on one particular stimulus or source of information while ignoring all others in the environment. Understanding this definition is important because there are two main forms of attention.

The first is top-down, or voluntary attention, which is based on "task demands" like needing to read a page in a textbook or solve a math problem. On the other side of the coin you've got bottom-up, or stimulus-driven, attention. Just like it sounds, this is automatically focused attention due to stimuli in the environment – SQUIRREL.

When you use your top-down attention to focus on something, your brain activates inhibitory mechanisms to block out competing stimuli. It can't do this forever, though; these mechanisms eventually tire just like the muscles in our body, and this leads to something called Directed Attention Fatigue. This is part of what causes you to become more and more distracted and less able to focus on your work as time goes by.

The strength of your inhibitory mechanisms, and hence your ability to focus on one task intensely, is variable. It depends on lots of different factors, including: - Your environment - Your personal tendency to seek novelty when faced with a boring or difficult task - Your interest in the task itself - Your brain's current state, which is dependent on the amount of fuel or food you've got, rest, exercise, anxiety, and a lot of different factors. - How long you've already been focusing your attention.

With that in mind, let's look at several different things that you can do to strengthen your attention muscle and also give it as much ammunition as it can get to focus well on whatever task you need to finish.

Stop Multi-Tasking

Many people try to deny it, but your brain can't actually do two things at once. Think of your brain like a single-core processor in a computer. These types of processors don't truly do multiple things at once – they just create the illusion of multi-tasking by rapidly switching from one task to another. So while you may think you're simultaneously watching YouTube videos and looking at pictures of cats your computer is actually just jumping back and forth between each.

But your brain is not good at doing this, which is why when you switch your attention from one task to another, you incur a cognitive switching penalty. Not only do you lose the raw amount of time it takes to switch from one task to another, but you also lose the amount of time it takes for your brain to properly refocus its attention and get back into the flow of things. And this can take quite a while, both because our brains simply take time to truly focus on a task in the first place, but also because switching from one task to another creates attention residue.

As the author Cal Newport explains in his book Deep Work: "...when you switch from some Task A to another Task B, your attention doesn't immediately follow— a residue of your attention remains stuck thinking about the original task."

This also happens when you switch from the task you're supposed to be focusing on over to a distraction, and then go back to the task after a few minutes. As you try to get back into the flow of your work, you'll be contending with the attention residue from cute cat videos you've watched on YouTube.

So, when you sit down and decide to work, choose one task and make it your only focus. You don't have to sit there and work on it until people mistake you for a hat rack, but do spend at least 20 or 30 minutes on it before switching to something else.

Tailor Your Environment for Better Focus

Start by finding a spot, either in your room or somewhere else, that you use ONLY for studying. By doing this, you're establishing a spot for yourself that has just one context, and context is powerful.

When your location, the people you're around, and all the other pieces of your environment point to a single activity, you'll be much more likely to do it. When you're in the gym, your brain knows you're there to work out. And even if you don't do it, it won't be because you're sitting there trying to decide between doing a set of pull-ups and doing your laundry.

A lot of great artists understand this, and they deliberately find or create spaces that are only for work. Some choose to work in cafes, like Nicholson's Cafe in Edinburgh, where J.K. Rowling wrote much of her first book, and some create isolated work spaces in their own homes, like the author Steven Pressfield.

Those examples highlight another important point, actually – there is no formula for a perfect study spot. It would seem like a silent, totally isolated desk in the basement of a library would put the least amount of strain on those inhibitory mechanisms, but as J.K. Rowling can attest, some people actually work better in a noisy coffee shop.

So you might need to experiment a bit before you find the context that works best for you. In general, though, the fewer things that are competing for your attention, the better.

Once you've chosen your spot, prepare it for your current task by putting away anything non-essential. This includes removing books and supplies that are unrelated, closing any tabs or programs you don't need, and putting away your phone.

When you're doing this, it can also be helpful to break your current task down into smaller chunks in order to decide what's essential to have out. The act of writing a research paper is a good example here; if you just think, "I have to write a paper," and then prep your study space for that task, then you'll have the internet open the whole time so you can do research.

But in reality, you can break that task down into several phases – brainstorming, researching, drafting, and editing. And once you do that, you'll realize you only need the internet for that research phase. During all the other ones, you can close it and cut its potential for being a distraction. All those cats are still going to be there later, I promise.

Also, anticipate potential distractions that might come up and try to get ahead of them. Maybe put your phone on do not disturb so no one can text you, or tell your friends you're studying and ask them not to bother you for a while. Anything you can do to mitigate future distractions will help you to stay focused and finish your work faster.

Once your study environment is established, the next area you should look to improve is your actual ability to focus. As we talked about before, your attention is like a muscle; it's something you can train over time to get stronger. One of the best ways to do this is by learning to resist cravings for novelty.

These are the sudden urges you get to check Snapchat or watch video of a corgi jumping into a lake while you're working on your English homework. You get these cravings because, by default, your brain doesn't like boredom or hard work. But the strength of these cravings is set by how often you give into them.

Our actions create habits and expectations in our brains, and these become hard-wired patterns of behavior. And this means that every time you give into that craving for a distraction, you're ingraining that decision as a habit. Luckily, you can also train the opposite behavior.

By acknowledging a craving for novelty, and then deliberately ignoring it and getting back to work, you start to build a tolerance for boredom and wean yourself off of that need for constant stimulation. As you do this, your ability to focus on your work strengthens. You're building that attention muscle.

Doing this is easier said than done – especially at first. However, there are tools you can use to give your brain some extra firepower in the early stages. Apps like Cold Turkey and StayFocusd can block distracting websites entirely, while a tool like Forest encourages you to ignore your phone by letting you grow virtual trees. And when you don't need a tool like the internet for your work, disconnecting it eliminates its potential for distraction entirely.

Of course, even with training, your brain's ability to focus still diminishes over time. Unlike computers, which are built to run all the time as long as they've got a steady supply of resources, our brains operate on a cycle of work and rest. Your circadian rhythm, which governs your sleep and wake cycle, is the best example – but it also applies on the smaller scale as well.

After a certain amount of work, you need to take a break. Now the amount of time will vary from person to person, but a good guideline to use is 25-30 minutes. Once you've spent that long on a task, if you feel your attention waning, take a break for a few minutes. Stand up, stretch, walk around a bit – maybe get some water.

During these short breaks, it's important not to switch to another task or get involved in something distracting, as you don't want to create that attention residue that makes it harder to get back into your work. After a few work sessions with these short breaks in between, you can then take a longer break to recharge. And during these longer breaks, it's fine to switch to something easier or do something fun for a little while – as long as you're planning in advance when these breaks will happen. That way, you're deliberately choosing when to work and when to indulge in distractions, rather than letting your mind be ruled by cravings for novelty.

Now, as time goes on, you'll probably find that you can go longer and longer before needing a break. This is a good sign that you're building those attention muscles. But realize that you'll always have a limited amount of focused energy you can expend in a day. Eventually, you've got to call it quits and go relax for a bit. And relaxation isn't the only thing your brain needs.

To keep being able to focus and improve long-term, you need to take care of your brain's biological needs as well. We often think of the brain as this non-physical, ethereal realm that isn't bound by the same limitations of our bodies. You know, "mind over matter" and all that stuff.

But your brain is still part of your body, which means that it needs plenty of sleep, nutrients, and exercise to work at peak efficiency. So if you're still struggling to focus, look at your health habits. Make sure you're getting at least 7 hours of sleep per night, eat healthy, and try to exercise once a day, even if it's just a short walk.

These things all take time, but – to quote Deep Work once again: High Quality Work = (Time Spent) x (Intensity of Focus) Taking care of your brain will allow you to focus more intensely when you do decide to work. Of course, making that decision to start working isn't always easy, which is why in the next chapter we'll be tackling what is probably the biggest problem students struggle with, which is procrastination.

Procrastination

Before we dive into specific solutions, it's useful to know why we procrastinate. Now, we could go deep on the biological battle between your prefrontal cortex and your limbic system, or in a million other directions, but since our focus is on solving the procrastination problem, one recent explanation that I find to be particularly useful is Temporal Motivation Theory, which is laid out by Dr. Piers Steele in his book The Procrastination Equation.

This theory suggests that a person's motivation to complete a task or assignment can be represented by an equation. And that equation is:

Motivation = (Expectancy * Value) / (Impulsiveness * Delay)

Now, while I don't really think all the complexities of human behavior can be boiled down into a neat little equation, I do think that this Procrastination Equation is a useful mental model for pinpointing the specific causes of our procrastination. So let's go ahead and break it down.

Expectancy is a term that represents how strongly you believe that you're able to complete a task, and it has an inverse correlation with your procrastination. If you feel competent at what you're doing, your expectancy will be high and that will increase your motivation to get to work. If the task looks really difficult, though, expectancy will be low and you'll be more likely to procrastinate.

The other place where you'll find that inverse correlation is between procrastination and Value, which includes the rewards you get for completing the task, as well as how pleasant – or unpleasant – the experience of actually doing it is.

Impulsiveness is how susceptible you are to distractions and, well, impulses to do other things, and it's directly correlated with procrastination. The less able you are to resist that sudden desire to go check Twitter, the more you're going to put off working on that English paper. And if you're thinking about going to check Twitter right now, remember: if you can resist that impulse, you'll actually be strengthening your brain's ability to focus. So fight it.

Finally, there's Delay, which is the amount of time between now and when you'll get the reward for completing the task.

The longer the delay is, the more you'll tend to procrastinate. This happens because human beings naturally place far more value on the short-term rather than long-term rewards – even if those long-term rewards are objectively greater. For most of human history, this was a helpful bit of brain programming.

If you were a hunter-gatherer living in 10,000 BCE, you had no reason to care about the antelopes you were going to hunt in 3 years – all that mattered was the one in front of you right now. But today, when your success in life depends more on studying for tests and remembering to put money in an IRA than on your antelope-hunting skills, your brain's hard-wired preference for short-term rewards becomes a hindrance.

It's the main reason why you consistently find yourself cramming for tests the night before; rationally, you know you should start studying a few weeks in advance, but most of your brain is like, "Eh, is that really necessary?" And to make matters worse, Delay is the hardest factor in the equation to control, since the time at which we'll get a task's reward is often set in stone. This is especially true when you're in school, since almost everything has a due date.

It's useful to simply be able to recognize that the delay between now and when you'll reap a task's reward matters a lot when it comes to your procrastination. And, really, that's the value of the equation as a whole; it's a mental model that makes it easy to pinpoint why you're procrastinating.

If it's because you feel like you're not skilled enough to actually complete the task, then you need to find a way to increase Expectancy. Or, if you notice that your attention is constantly being pulled in other directions, then it's time to figure out how to decrease your Impulsiveness.

So now let's go over some specific ideas for manipulating those three most malleable factors. To raise expectancy, you can do several things. One of the most helpful is to break the task down into smaller sub-tasks.

Doing this allows you to narrow your focus to something that's not nearly as daunting, and it also lets you more clearly define the specific actions you have to take. So if you're writing a paper, realize that "write a paper" is a project that can – and should – be broken down.

You've got the research phase, the rough draft phase – which you can break further down into sections, like the intro, arguments, and conclusion – and then you've got the editing phase. Once you've defined these actions and know what order to tackle them in, you'll have a much clearer vision of what should be done right now. Plus, writing the rough draft of an intro paragraph is much easier than trying to write the entire paper all at once.

Another great way to raise Expectancy is to simply ask for help. While being able to figure things out on your own is definitely a useful skill, there comes a point when refusing to reach out to someone else only slows you down. So go to your teacher's office hours, or find a friend to form a study group with.

Now when it comes to improving a task's Value, there are a few things you can do:

- Improve the actual reward for completing the task
- Improve the experience of doing the work itself
- Add additional rewards, or mini-rewards for completing sub-tasks

The best way to improve the first item on the list is to choose work that's more fulfilling to you.

You have some amount of control over this when you're selecting your classes, and as you move into your career and build up more experience, that amount of control will definitely increase. However, when you're a student, there are still a ton of required classes and things that you just have to do. And once you've started, it's pretty difficult to improve the actual reward – it's usually set in stone.

If you finish a math assignment, you'll get the credit for it and you'll improve your math skills. Pretty simple. But you do have a lot of control over the other two items. To make the experience of doing the work itself more pleasant, you could choose a study location that you enjoy being in – like a coffee shop or your favorite spot in the library. You can also find a good study music playlist, work with a friend, or go for a quick walk beforehand to raise your energy levels before you start. And additional rewards can further boost your motivation.

There are several ways to create these, including gamification, which is the idea of taking elements from games and applying them to your work. One of my favorite ways to do this is with Habitica, an app that essentially turns productivity into a role-playing game.

Habitica takes all the elements that make RPGs like Pokemon and Final Fantasy so addicting – levelling up, experience points, gear – and it applies them to real life. I use Habitica as a tool for sticking to my morning routine and making sure I work out enough, but there's also a to-do list function, which you can use for individual assignments and tasks.

If you don't want to do that, you can keep things simpler by just setting up small rewards for finishing sub-tasks – like letting yourself watch a movie or go out with friends after you finish taking notes on a couple of sources for that research paper you're working on.

It's here that I want to talk about the concept of **low-density fun vs. high-density fun**. See, a lot of students feel like they have too much work to ever let themselves do anything fun that takes a significant amount of time. Maybe you've had these kinds of thoughts yourself, as well. You think, "Man, I'd really love to play Horizon Zero Dawn right now, but I should really use that time to study."

The irony is that these same students who are constantly denying themselves that high-density fun are also spending a lot of time checking Facebook, or picking new outfits for their Bitmoji avatars, or browsing memes.

These things represent low-density fun; they're more attractive than doing work, and it's easy to convince yourself that you're only going to do them for 5 minutes. But inevitably you do end up spending a ton of time on them – after all, these websites and apps are literally designed from the ground up to be as addictive as possible – and what's worse, they're not actually fun. They're just distractions.

And if you waste all your time on them, you leave no time for actual, high-density fun that can act as a true motivator for finishing your work. So the counterintuitive tip here is that you NEED to let yourself have this high-density fun. Give yourself two hours tonight to play that new video game. Or join that off-road dirt boarding club you've had your eye on. When you allow yourself to do these things, you create anticipation that can be used as focusing energy for your work.

And that brings us to Impulsiveness. If you're studying in a place where you have access to distractions, your attention is more likely to be pulled away by them. So find a dedicated study spot away from friends and away from video games. Sometimes, you might even need to lock that environment down a bit.

One thing that the Procrastination Equation doesn't cover is the role that willpower plays in procrastination. For a long time, it was believed that willpower was a limited resource – and that it drained throughout the day as you made decisions that deviated from the path of least resistance. This phenomenon was called ego depletion.

During the past couple of years, though, the ego depletion theory been challenged by some conflicting research, so it's tough to say whether or not willpower itself really is this limited pool that you draw from throughout the day. Ego depletion controversy aside, though, your body – and, by extension, your brain – runs on a cycle of work and rest. There's only so much you can do in a day before you exhaust your mental resources.

Plus, when you put off a challenging assignment in favor of doing a bunch of easy work first, it becomes really easy to convince yourself that you've "done enough" for the day once that easy work is done. That's why one of the best ways to beat procrastination is to just knuckle down and do the most difficult, unpleasant thing on your to-do list first.

This is often called "eating the frog" – and as Mark Twain once said: "If it's your job to eat a frog, it's best to do it first thing in the morning. And If it's your job to eat two frogs, it's best to eat the biggest one first."

I'd much rather eat a tomato, which in Italian would be called a "pomodoro" – and that happens to be the name of the final technique we're going to discuss today. **The Pomodoro Technique** is a simple little hack you can use to stop procrastinating, and all it requires is a timer and a little piece of paper. To use it, first decide on one singular task you're going to work on. Then, set your timer for 25 minutes, and work as hard as you can on that task during that time. If a distraction comes up, or if you get the impulse to do something else, write it down on the piece of paper and then get back to work. Finally, once the timer goes off, take a 5-minute break and then repeat the process until you're ready for a longer break.

This method works so well because the timer helps you to reframe your task as input-based rather than output-based. Instead of feeling like you need to finish an entire math assignment or that rough draft of your paper, you know you just need to work for 25 minutes. This act of reframing cuts down on the initial resistance you feel towards the task, since 25 minutes of work doesn't feel like a huge investment of effort.

Additionally, the timer creates an external motivator. Instead of relying on your brain to keep track of how long you should work, you let the timer do it for you. It's the next best thing to having a coach or drill instructor there to keep you on task – and for that reason, you need to make sure you actually use a timer – or at least a timer app.

There comes a point where talking about productivity becomes a form of procrastination itself, so now it's time to take what you've learned in this chapter, apply it, and get to work. Good luck.

Studying for Exams

Benjamin Franklin once took a few seconds out of his busy schedule to remark, "By failing to prepare, you are preparing to fail." This is doubly true when it comes to preparing for your exams.

So in this chapter I am going to guide you through the process of creating a study schedule, reviewing effectively so that you master the material, and doing it all without cracking under the pressure

As we've previously discussed, learning takes time. Encoding new information into solid memories is a physical process that doesn't happen overnight, and it requires multiple exposures or recollections which need to be spaced out.

But, as we've also discussed, your brain isn't built to make long-term focused decisions. It's hard-wired to care a lot more about now than later.

Study Schedule

What this all means is that the structure of the stuff sitting up in your cranium isn't up to the task of preparing for a test – so you need to build external structures to help it out. And, arguably, the most important one is a study schedule. I recommend building your study schedule directly into the calendar you're already using for everything else, as it's crucial to figure out how you're going to balance your time between studying and finishing all the assignments and homework that lead up to the test.

The first step to doing this is to figure out the exact dates and times of your exams, and then to add them to your calendar. In my Google Calendar, I actually have a specific calendar that's colored differently from all other events, and that lets me see those dates and times at a glance. I'd also make sure to include the location for any exam that's being held somewhere other than that class's normal room – which happened pretty often for me in college.

Once those dates are safely stored in your calendar, work backwards and schedule study sessions during the 3 or 4 weeks leading up to your exams if they're finals. If it's a smaller exam, two weeks will probably do. If you've got a lot of homework or group projects, try to schedule time to work on those as well.

When it comes time to actually sit down and study, try to replicate the test conditions as much as you possibly can. Memory is very context-based, so if you can review the material under conditions that are similar to those of the test, recalling it will be much easier when you're actually taking it. So, how do you do this?

Well, first try to get as much information about the test as possible. Ask your teacher – or look at the syllabus – to find out what material will be covered, whether or not the test will be comprehensive, how many questions there will be, and how long you'll have to answer them. You'll also want to know what types of questions you'll be up against – will they be multiple choice, true/false, short answer, or essay?

Lastly, don't forget to ask about what materials will be allowed, such as scratch paper or calculators. Once you have all those details locked down, the next step is to try to get your hands on practice tests, or tests from previous semesters.

You can ask your teacher if they have any that they're willing to give out as review material, and if you're in college, there might be a fraternity, or sorority, or some other student organization that keeps a test bank you can dig through. There's also an online test bank at Koofers.com that contains old tests from lots of universities, so that's worth a look as well.

Now that you've gathered all of your resources, it's time to study. But where should you do it? While most of your studying will probably happen in your established study space, you should also try to do at least one or two sessions in the actual classroom you'll be tested in – or at least some other classroom with a similar look and feel.

As I mentioned earlier, memory is context-dependent. Our brains are better able to recall things they've learned when we're in a similar context to the one in which we originally learned or reviewed the material.

In fact, one study published in 1975 demonstrated how subjects who learned lists of vocabulary words underwater in scuba diving gear were much more easily able to recall those words when they went back underwater again, as opposed to when they were on dry land.

Don't stop at the location, though. Also spend some time studying under the same constraints that you'll have during the test. Set a timer to simulate the test's time limit, and quiz yourself without having access to your textbook, notes, or any other materials that you won't have during the test.

And notice that I said "quiz yourself" here. The best way to study for a test is to do it actively and to focus on recall – to force yourself to actually pull facts and answers up from the depths of your memory banks.

At this point you might be thinking to yourself, "This all sounds good BUT how am I supposed to quiz myself in the first place – especially if my teacher didn't give me any practice tests?" Well, you make your own quizzes, of course.

Now, if your teacher gave you a study guide, then that's going to be your #1 resource for creating these quizzes. Just take every concept listed on the guide and convert it into a question. If you don't happen to have one of those, then do the same thing with your lecture notes. Look through them and create questions out of headings, main concepts, and even case studies.

When you're forming your questions, in general you're going to want to emulate the test as much as possible. However, there are a few types of questions that lend themselves perfectly to certain formats. For example, facts and vocabulary terms are great candidates for flash cards.

Studying flash cards is another form of quizzing yourself, and they have one great benefit – you can study them from both sides. If you're studying for a chemistry exam, one card can ask you what the chemical symbol for Neon is, and if you flip it over, it can also make sure you know what Ne represents. This ensures that your brain can make the connection no matter where it starts.

When it comes to subjects like math or physics, where your questions will usually take the form of equations or problems, you want to spend the majority of your study time actually working through those problems. Spend a little bit of time familiarizing yourself with formulas and concepts, sure, but spend way more time practicing and making sure you can actually perform the operations yourself.

How to Ask Your Teacher for Help

As you spend time actively solving these problems, you're inevitably going to run into things you don't know how to solve. When you do, it's important to know when to ask your teacher for help – and how to do it correctly.

Dale Corson, the 8th dean of Cornell University and a professor of chemistry, offered some advice to his students for how to effectively ask for help. Before going up to the professor, he said, ask yourself: What is it –

exactly – that I don't understand? This obvious-sounding piece of advice is worth stating plainly because, as Corson puts it, many students would come up and say – with a general sweep of the hand – "I don't get this."

The moment they encountered a tough spot, they'd disengage and let their brain essentially give up. Don't do this. When you become confused, spend 15 more minutes trying to solve the problem on your own. Work line by line through the problem until you know precisely where the confusion begins.

Also, try to write down the solutions you've tried so far. Doing this essentially documents the problem and creates context for the person who will eventually help you – and it might actually help you solve the problem on your own as well.

In the world of software development, programmers who are stuck on broken pieces of code will often use a technique called Rubber Duck Debugging, which involves explaining the code and thought process behind it to a rubber duck. The idea here is that explaining the problem to a non-expert – in this case, a cute little duck on your desk – forces you to think about it from a different perspective, which will often reveal the solution.

Additionally, going through this process will show your teacher that you've truly put in some effort and aren't just coming to them for help out of laziness. And that's a great way to earn their respect.

Index Cards

Now, if you want another really effective way to solidify the material quickly, do a cheat card exercise. Remember that really cool teacher that once let you write whatever you wanted on an index card and bring it with you into a test? Because I do, and in my book, that teacher was almost as cool as the one who let us play with magnesium and bunsen burners unsupervised – for science, of course.

Most teachers aren't going to let you bring a cheat card into the exam – but that shouldn't stop you from making one. The thing about an index card is that it's small. And even though I pushed the limits of how tiny a human hand can write whenever I got the opportunity to make a cheat card, there's only so much I could fit on it. And due to that limitation, I had to be very choosy about what I put on the card – which resulted in a tiny piece of cardstock containing the most important information on the exam.

Since I'd just spent an hour looking all that stuff up and writing it down in teeny tiny letters, I was interacting with it – actively – the whole time. That's the beauty of a cheat card exercise. Even if you can't bring your card with you into the test, you spend a concentrated block of time selecting and writing down the most crucial information. It's a great preparation technique.

Not Studying

Speaking of great preparation techniques, the last one we're going to cover is not studying. At least some of the time. Students often believe that they should be spending all of their time studying if they want to do well, but remember: how well you do is determined by the both the time you put in and the intensity of your focus.

And to enable your brain to focus intensely, you have to give it some time off. The cycle of work and rest has to be respected. So when you're crafting your study schedule, give yourself time for breaks. That includes short breaks during review sessions, as well as some longer periods where you can de-stress and reward yourself with some of that good old high-density fun. Doing this will ensure that you're alert, attentive, and happy – well, as happy as somebody with a calculus final coming up can be.

And if you're creating your study schedule well in advance, you should have no problem giving yourself time for these breaks while also leaving enough hours open for studying.

Test Anxiety

Henry Fonda was a famous actor with a career that spanned 54 years and included starring roles in classic movies like 12 Angry Men and Once Upon a Time in the West. He was one of the most well-known and successful actors of his time, bringing home an Oscar, two Golden Globes, and even a Grammy before retiring. So it might surprise you to learn that Fonda had a lifelong struggle with performance anxiety.

In fact, even when he was 75 years old, with over half a century of acting experience under his belt, he would often throw up before beginning stage performances. But, despite his anxiety and sudden lack of lunch, Fonda would still step out from behind the curtain and give the audience the great performance they expected. That's because he understood one of the unavoidable facts of life – a fact that the author Steven Pressfield put so well in his book The War of Art: "Fear doesn't go away. The warrior and the artist live by the same code of necessity, which dictates that the battle must be fought anew every day."

If you're a student, you might not be performing on a stage or facing down an enemy army, but your tests and exams are battles all their own, and they often come with the same feelings of anxiety. These feelings are normal, and you'll never truly banish them. If you're doing work that's important to you, you'll always feel some amount of anxiety.

And that can actually be a good thing, because anxiety is an indicator that what you're doing IS important. Otherwise, you'd be apathetic about it. However, too much test anxiety can hurt you.

Research has shown that high-pressure situations can actually deplete your working memory. Additionally, stress caused by anxiety produces a hormone called cortisol, and too much cortisol can hinder the ability of the hippocampus to recall memories. This means that it is crucial to learn how to manage your test anxiety.

You have to learn how to perform well in the face of it, and make sure it doesn't consume your thoughts so you can actually solve that geometry proof that's staring you in the face. Fortunately, there are several techniques and mental exercises you can use to do that.

Test anxiety is caused by many different factors, but today we're going to focus on the most common ones, which I call the Three Big Fears:

- A fear of repeating past failures
- The fear of the unknown
- The fear of the stakes

Before we figure out how you can combat these fears, there is one general purpose strategy I want to share with you. The next time you feel anxious going into a test, take out a piece of paper and spend a couple minutes writing out exactly what's causing you to feel that way. This has been scientifically proven to reduce test anxiety.

A study done at the University of Chicago found that students who were given 10 minutes to write about their fears and anxieties before a test improved their scores by an average of nearly one grade point compared to the control group. This technique works for pretty much the same reason that using a to-do list works: It allows you to take all those worries out of your head and store them somewhere safe.

You've probably been in a situation before where you're stressed, and a friend tells you, "Hey, just don't worry about it, man!" Of course, you can't – right? You can't just let go of the things that are worrying you – after all, your brain thinks they're important.

However, by writing them down, you're unloading those worries into an external system that you trust. Subconsciously, you know that they're not going anywhere. And by doing this, you free up mental resources that you can then devote to doing well on the test.

So that brings us to our first big fear: **the fear of repeating past failures**. Logically, everyone knows that failure is inevitable every once in a while. "To err is human," wrote Alexander Pope, and the realm of calculus finals is no exception. But we're not always logical.

In fact, human beings have an inherent negativity bias – a tendency to remember and give more emotional weight to negative events rather than positive ones. This is a feature of the brain that's pretty useful when it comes to survival – after all, remembering which mushrooms made you sick or not to try to shake hands with a tiger is pretty important for survival.

But the negativity bias doesn't limit itself to poisonous mushrooms or tigers; any negative event can create feelings of apprehension and fear when it comes up again. So even though almost everyone does poorly on tests and exams at least once in a while, when it happens to you, you might naturally fear that it'll happen again the next time around. So how you do you actually beat this negativity bias?

Well, first, realize that you're not defined by your past successes or failures – despite what that insidious part of your brain might try to tell you. While the path you're on right now is certainly in part a product of your past choices, it's not a path with a predetermined destination.

At any time, you can choose to do things differently than you did in the past. If you're ready to do that, you need to start by analysing your past mistakes and gathering as much information about them as you can. After all, you can only improve if you know what you were doing wrong before.

Elite chess players understand this concept really well. While they spend a lot of their practice time playing games and studying the openings and endgames of players at higher ranks, they also dedicate a ton of time to analysing their own past games – especially the ones they lost.

By doing so, they can start to correct bad habits and uncover patterns in their playing, which can then be tweaked or improved in the future. So take a cue from these chess players – as well as from elite performers in pretty much any other discipline, be it opera singers or figure skaters – and review your past exams to see how you can improve.

Start by getting your hands on a copy of your past exam; if your teacher doesn't usually hand these out or let you take them home, talk to them after class and ask if you can at least look it over. And while you're talking with them, also ask for feedback – especially if your exam contained short-answer or essay questions where there's no concrete answer.

Once you've got a past exam in your hands, review the mistakes you made. Don't just acknowledge your mistakes; for each incorrect question, make sure you understand why your answer was the wrong one. If it was a complex problem – like a math equation – identify the exact point where you made a mistake. Additionally, make sure you know what the right answer was, and why it was right.

Before you move on, cross-reference the question with your notes, as well. If you're going to be tested on that question again – like in a final exam – highlight that section of your notes so you know it's important. You can also create quiz questions for later review. Overall, shoot for mastery over the material so you don't make the same mistake again.

The details of those incorrect questions aren't the only things that deserve reflection. You also need to figure out why you made the mistakes in the first place. Ask yourself: Was I unprepared? And if so, why was I unprepared? Did I simply not put enough time into reviewing? Did I ignore the study guide? Or did I use an ineffective study method?

If you feel that you were prepared, then maybe something went wrong during the actual exam. Maybe you rushed through and made a lot of careless errors. Or maybe you let time get away from you and didn't actually finish the whole exam. Or maybe that creepy AI from Ghost in the Shell hacked your brain in the middle of the exam and forced you to spend the whole time licking your paper. These things happen.

Whatever the reason was, don't let it get you down too much. Remember that failure is a great teacher – and it's a better one than success. Since we remember our failures so well, every one of them is a lesson and an opportunity. But you need to make sure that you use that opportunity by making a plan for how you'll avoid the mistake in the future.

Just saying "I'll do better next time" isn't enough – you need to know exactly how you're going to do better. And that's not all you need to know. In fact, the more you can learn about your exam in all its facets, the more comfortable you're going to be.

This is the way to overcome the second of our big fears: **The Fear of the Unknown**. People naturally fear what they don't understand, and in general, this is a good thing! It's another one of those pieces of brain programming that's useful for survival, and most other animals share it with us.

When I visited New York City for the first time several years ago, I noticed that the squirrels there seemed much less afraid of people than the squirrels back home – but that was because these big-city squirrels had a lot of experience dealing with people, and it was mostly positive.

So try to gain as much experience with the upcoming exam as you can. Now, we talked a lot about how to do this in the last video on preparing for tests, but the general principle is to try to replicate the test conditions when you're studying. Do your best to get access to practice tests and study guides, and create quizzes out of your notes to fill in the gaps.

Additionally, spend some time studying in a classroom that looks and feels similar to the one you'll be tested in, and quiz yourself under the same time constraints that you'll face during the exam. You want to make the test feel like a familiar old friend when you actually face it.

As Scott Berkun, a professional public speaker, put it: "By the time I present to an actual audience, it's not really the first time at all." That's the feeling you're going for.

And that brings us to the last of our big three fears, which is the **Fear of the Stakes**. One of the biggest sources of test anxiety is the feeling that this test means everything – it's going to define your overall grade, where you'll be able to go to college, and whether or not you'll get to work for Elon Musk someday.

But in reality, you're rarely going to come across a test or situation that you can't recover from in the case that things go wrong. Trust me – I actually failed a test in college once. And, even worse, I was once fired from a job.

In both cases it was totally my fault, but I learned my lessons, I made sure I never made the same mistakes again, and I moved on. And even if things don't go perfectly for you, you'll be able to do the same thing. If that's not comforting enough, try reframing the test in your mind.

Think of it as yet another learning opportunity rather than as a judgement. After all, a test challenges you to recall what you've learned, and as we've already discussed, active recall strengthens your mastery over the material. And – at least for me – viewing a test this way makes it seem a lot less scary.

Lastly, keep in your mind that anxiety isn't something you always need to try to deal with on your own. If you have anxiety that's majorly affecting your life, don't hesitate to ask a professional for help.

Papers and Essays

Let's be real here – you've got a 2,000-word essay due in less than 24 hours and you've probably been scrolling through Instagram for the past hour. Leave Instagram alone it's time to write that paper.

Simon Peyton Jones, a researcher for Microsoft, once gave a talk at Cambridge University about how to write a great research paper. In this talk, he advised the audience to start out the paper writing process with a pre-writing phase. Only once that's done should they go to research.

Most people do this in the opposite way. They get their idea, they go do a bunch of research on it, and then write their paper. But I like Jones' advice to go through a pre-writing phase before doing any research, because it does a couple of very important things.

First, pre-writing will dredge up things you didn't even think you knew about the topic. This is something that professional writers know really well; when you spend some quality time writing in a focused state, your brain will make connections and serve up memories you didn't even know you had. As a result, you'll come up with lots of great questions and preliminary arguments that might just make it into your final draft.

And this leads directly to the second benefit, which is more focused research. When you go into the research process armed with questions and arguments from your pre-writing phase, you'll have a much better idea of what you're looking for, and you'll spend a lot less time going down pointless rabbit holes.

The first thing to understand about the pre-writing phase is that it's not about cranking out a polished paper on your first try. For one, you haven't even done the research yet – but more importantly, a paper is a big project. And with big projects, you need to just jump in and make a mess at first.

It's like an artist creating a sculpture out of a solid block of marble. Any good artist knows that it's much easier to hammer out the basic features right away instead of trying to jump right into the detailed work. And at first, the result will be a mess, but it's much easier to hone a mess into something great than to turn a solid block of marble into a masterpiece on the first pass.

So let's get into the details. Personally, my pre-writing phase usually takes the form of a brain dump. Now, this is not an attempt to write a coherent paper. Instead, it's just a chance for me to get all of my thoughts onto a piece of paper or into a document in my note-taking app. When I do a brain dump, I'll open a new document, set a timer for 25 minutes, like we talked about in the procrastination chapter, and then I just start writing.

Specifically, I'm looking to pull basically everything I know about the topic out of my brain, as well as identify any questions I might have. I'll also list out any main points that I think will be important to cover, and finally try to think of any specific external resources that might be useful to look at during the research process.

Once you've done a brain dump, it's time to move onto the research process. Now, the biggest pitfall that most students deal with here is the tendency to get stuck in this phase forever.

The author Cal Newport calls this "research recursion syndrome" – you get stuck in a loop of constantly looking for yet another source. In his book How to Become a Straight-A Student, Newport lays out an algorithm of sorts for ensuring you don't get stuck in this loop. First, you find your sources.

You'll probably find most of these at the library or on the internet. A safe place that you might actually want to start with is Wikipedia. Some of your teachers are going to say that Wikipedia isn't a good source – and they're right.

However, the citations section at the bottom of each and every Wikipedia article is actually a really great place to find good sources, since Wikipedia holds their articles to high standards and requires high-quality source material – like scientific studies published in reputable journals.

Aside from Wikipedia, though, you'll also find lots of good sources through Google Scholar, journal databases like EBSCO, your school library, and – one place you might not have thought of before – the notes or bibliography section in most popular science books. For example, Bill Bryson's book A Short History of Nearly Everything contains 48 pages of citations and references to other works.

Once you've found your sources, make personal copies of them – create photocopies if they're in books or other paper formats, or add them to a note-taking app if they're digital. This ensures that you'll always have them available to you when you're writing without having to go look them up again.

Next, you want to annotate the material. Skim each source, highlight the sections that you feel are specifically relevant to the arguments you want to make, and add any notes that might help you hammer out the details of those arguments when you're actually writing the final draft.

Finally, consciously ask yourself if you're done. Cal's ballpark suggestion here is to have at least two sources for each main point in your thesis, and at least one for any tangential or non-crucial points. Of course, this is a general suggestion, so you'll have to make the final call. If the answer is no, repeat the process. If the answer is yes, then it's time to write your first real draft. And this should be an awful first draft.

There's a popular adage that's often attributed to Ernest Hemingway which goes, "Write drunk, edit sober." Now, there are a more than a few things wrong with this quote. First, Hemingway never said it – it's actually a pithy re-phrasing of a passage from a novel called Reuben, Reuben by Peter De Vries.

Secondly, Hemingway definitely didn't write this way – even though he was a guy who definitely drank a lot in his spare time. However, it's still a useful piece of advice as long as it isn't taken literally.

What's it's actually getting at is the usefulness of letting the initial act of creation be free of scrutiny and restraint. And this is important, because one of the most difficult problems that writers deal with is perfectionism.

It's ok if your first draft is awful, because future you will be there to edit it and shape it into something great.

One technique that I've found to be helpful during this process is to write my first draft in a different place than where I intend the final draft to go. This might be a separate document, or it might be an entirely different app.

For instance, I write the first draft of almost every one of my blog posts and video scripts in Evernote. Later, I'll polish them up in Google Drive. Using a separate app helps me to truly believe that it's ok to make a mess. Of course, that mess has to get cleaned up eventually!

I did say that cleaning it up is future you's problem, but eventually future you will become now you. So let's talk about editing.

I recommend editing your paper in two separate stages. Stage one is the **content edit**. Here, you're looking at your paper as a whole and asking yourself the most important questions: Does each argument support the thesis? Does the paper have a good narrative flow? Is each argument properly fleshed out and backed up with research or external sources? What can be removed or written in a clearer, simpler way?

Essentially, this stage is all about making sure the paper communicates your message to the reader as effectively as possible. It's not about spelling errors. Those you should save for stage two – the **technical edit**.

At this point, you're ready to go over your paper with a fine-toothed comb to identify any problems with the structure or syntax. Things like:

- Spelling and grammar mistakes
- Poorly structured sentences
- Formatting errors
- Sentences that just don't sound right

I find that the most effective way to do a technical edit is to print out the paper and go over it by hand. It's just easier to catch mistakes when you're editing the paper in its final intended medium. Plus, by using pen and paper, you're prevented from making corrections on the fly. Doing so would require switching contexts from editing to writing, which can be fatiguing and makes it easier to get sloppy near the end of the paper.

In addition to printing out your paper, you should also take the time to read it out loud. This forces you to slow down and prevents you from unconsciously skipping over any words, and it also helps you identify any sentences that don't sound good.

Finally, remember that one set of eyes isn't good enough – especially when they're your own. To make your paper truly great, you need to let other people look over it and get their feedback.

First, realize that each person can only read your paper for the first time exactly once. Nobody can read your paper with fresh eyes twice. So be strategic with your reviewers. Let a couple people read the first draft, and keep other people on deck for the final one.

Secondly, make sure to explicitly ask for the kind of feedback you actually want. When people aren't given direction, they'll naturally gravitate to looking for spelling and grammar errors – which aren't nearly as important as the big elements, like whether your arguments even make sense. Finally, after you've gotten your feedback and finished both stages of editing, print out your final draft and give it one final read-through from start to finish.

If everything makes sense and nothing sticks out as glaringly wrong, give yourself permission to be done. In all likelihood, you've just crafted an excellent paper. Congrats!

Exercise

Over the course of this book, we've covered the topics such as– preparing for tests, planning, beating procrastination, and so on. In this chapter we're going to step slightly out of that realm of study related content to talk about exercise. But don't be fooled – this will still help you to become a better student.

Exercise is crucial for keeping both your body and your brain healthy, and as you'll see later in this video, it's also a simple way to improve your ability to learn and focus. The problem is that our culture is becoming less and less active.

Here in the U.S., nearly a third of kids between the ages of 2 and 19 qualifies as either overweight or obese. And on average, we spend over 10 hours a day looking at screens – an activity that almost always involves sitting down. And many schools aren't helping the issue, as physical education programs are constantly being cut in favor of adding more time to other classes.

In this chapter we're going to dive deep into the brain benefits of exercise. And keep in mind here that we're not talking about a narrow definition of exercise, like lifting weights or running. Exercise comes in many different shapes and forms, and regardless of your skill level or physical limitations, you can probably find something that gets your heart rate up – which can, in turn, improve your mind.

When we think about the concept of "learning", we often picture someone lost in some kind of intellectual work – doing research, reading a book, or maybe working through a bunch of math problems. But it's important to realize that all of these activities are relatively recent inventions when looked at on an evolutionary time scale.

For the vast majority of the time that the brain has been around – be it inside the skull of a human or something else – its ability to learn evolved right alongside movement. And this makes sense if you think about it.

Lifeforms that don't need to move really have no use for a brain. Plants just need to take root in one spot and then grow upward, and for that, a fixed set of genetic programming will do just fine. The ability to learn, think, and strategize only becomes necessary when you can move around, because now you need to be able to navigate a complex environment, find food and remember its location later on, and escape from predators.

If you want a good example of this difference, look at the sea squirt. These invertebrates start their lives in a larval stage complete with a primitive eye, a tail-like nerve cord that lets them move around, and a brain. At this stage, their goal is to find a spot on the ocean floor where they can attach themselves.

Once they do this, that's where they'll be staying for the rest of their lives. And to seal the deal, they absorb all of those useful features that let them move around – the eye, the nerve cord, and – you guessed it – the brain. That's right – once a sea squirt doesn't need to move anymore, it basically eats its own brain.

The neuroscientist Rodolfo Llinás used the case of the brain-eating sea squirt in his book I of the Vortex: From Neurons to Self in order to illustrate his conclusion that: "That which we call thinking is the evolutionary internalization of movement."

In other words, brains are for creatures that move. Once you stop using it, you lose it. In fact, "use it or lose it," is a principle that applies to much of biology – not just brains. That's why your muscles can start to atrophy if you don't use them for long enough, and why failing to stay active and learn new things can greatly increase the risk of developing dementia as you get older.

To use an even more extreme example, astronauts that spend a lot of time in orbit often suffer from a condition called spaceflight osteopenia, which is a loss in bone density that happens because the skeleton doesn't have to constantly fight against the pull of Earth's gravity. On the whole, every part of your body is adapted to allow you to do specific things. If you aren't doing them, then those parts of your body simply become resource hogs.

But you can't just decide you don't need them and turn them off – your body's systems are highly connected and they depend on each other, which means that you need to do what your body is built to do if you want to keep it all working.

And in the case of exercise, it's not just a matter of "working" or "not working" – in addition to keeping you healthy, getting your heartbeat elevated on a regular basis can also make you a better student. Just look at the school district of Naperville, Illinois.

Back in the year 1990, a P.E. teacher in Naperville named Phil Lawler decided that the traditional structure of P.E. classes just wasn't going to cut it anymore. Since they were almost always based on sports, the few kids who were already athletic would naturally dominate the more active roles, and by consequence, lots of other kids would end up just standing around – not really doing much at all.

Lawler decided to change things up, and he shifted his class's focus from traditional sports to more fitness-based activities like jogging. He placed an emphasis on constant movement and keeping heart rates in an elevated zone during the entire period. And – most importantly – he graded his students on effort rather than skill.

By using heart rate monitors, he was able to tell that students who clocked 10-minute mile times were still working just as hard as those who could finish in 8. He called this program Zero Hour P.E., and it started as an optional morning program before becoming integrated into the school's normal schedule.

By the end of its first semester in 1990, his test group of students showed a 17% improvement in reading and comprehension, compared to a 10.7% average improvement for the kids who didn't participate. After that, the structure of Zero Hour P.E. became the archetype for the entire district's physical education program.

And today, the district consistently ranks in the state's top 10 academic performers, even though money spent per student there is much lower than other top-tier districts. The correlation between fitness-based P.E. classes and higher grades isn't limited to Naperville, either.

After studying Lawler's program, another P.E. teacher named Tim McCord brought it to his own school district in Titusville, Pennsylvania. And in 2008, eight years after the program had started there, the district's reading scores had gone from below the state average to 17% above it.

Likewise, math scores went from below the average to 18% above it. So what's going on here? How exactly does exercise help you become a better student? Well, broadly speaking, regular exercise improves your brain in three important ways.

First, it optimizes the levels of neurotransmitters like serotonin, norepinephrine, and dopamine. These are all crucial for learning. Keep in mind that we are hugely oversimplifying things here, but in general, serotonin helps to regulate your mood and keeps you happy. Norepinephrine amplifies signals related to attention and motivation, and dopamine is highly involved in learning, movement, and operating the brain's reward center. Regular exercise balances these neurotransmitters, along with lots of others that are equally important for keeping your brain healthy.

Secondly, exercise can also stimulate neurogenesis, which is the birth of new neurons from neural stem cells in the hippocampus. This was once thought to be impossible. For a long time, the prevailing belief in the scientific community was that you were born with all the neurons you were ever going to get. But we now know that new neurons are created even during adulthood, and exercise increases their rate of creation.

One important thing to note here is that these new neurons are born as stem cells that don't have an immediate purpose. As a result, many of them die – again, "use it or lose it." In order for a new neuron to survive, it has to get plugged into an existing neural network, and that happens when you learn new things. So really, the crucial combo for this particular bit of brain optimization is regular exercise AND constant learning.

If you're a student, you've probably got the second part down pat at the moment, but I do want to mention this, since it remains true even as you get older and eventually don't have to go to school anymore.

Lastly, exercise improves the ability of neurons to bind to one another, which is how new neural pathways are formed and how memories take hold. It does this by promoting the production of a protein called brain-derived neurotrophic factor (or BDNF), which in turn enables and improves a process called long-term potentiation. This is the mechanism that enables learning. When new information enters your brain, neurons start firing using existing stores of another neurotransmitter called glutamate.

If the firing continues, each active neuron will also start generating building material for the creation of brand new synapses, which are connections between separate neurons. As these new synapses are created, memories form. And BDNF is the secret sauce that makes the whole process possible.

In fact, researchers have discovered that depriving rats of BDNF causes them to lose the capacity for long-term potentiation. And, on the flip side, they've also found that injecting BDNF directly into a rat's brain increases that capacity.

This does not mean that you should go ask your doctor to inject BDNF in your brain – they're probably going to give you a pretty weird look. And it's unnecessary anyway, because your brain naturally produces more BDNF when you learn new things and when you exercise.

There are also other benefits that go beyond learning; research has found that regular exercise can also improve your ability to focus and block out distractions, it reduces stress, and it lets you control the weather with your mind. We don't have time to dig into the details of these benefits here, but if you're curious, you can learn a lot more about each of them in Dr. John Ratey's book Spark: The Revolutionary New Science of Exercise and the Brain.

Except for that last one – I was lying about that one. What we need to do now is answer the million-dollar question: How, exactly, should you exercise if you want to improve your brain's performance? Well, first off, don't try to do traditional academic learning during intense exercise. You think it'd be a pretty sweet productivity hack to study your organic chemistry flash cards during a set of heavy deadlifts, but it's not going to work out so well.

When your heart rate is elevated, blood actually moves away from your prefrontal cortex, which manages your executive functions, working memory, and the intake of new information. However, that blood comes back almost immediately after you finish exercising, so doing a workout or going for a run right before you start learning is a great idea.

As for how you should exercise – well, that's mostly up to you, but you'll get the best results by combining an elevated heart rate with complex, skill-based movement. One way to do this is to opt for a sport or a skill-based activity that combines both, like figure skating, basketball, skateboarding, martial arts, or even intense yoga.

Alternatively, you can first do some aerobic exercise followed by a lower intensity bout of skill based movement, like going for a 15 minute run and then doing some rock climbing. But beyond all else, just get started. Even going for a short walk once a day can have a lot of benefits.

So if you're not getting a lot of exercise right now, just start small, do what you can do, and focus on building the habit. You don't need to worry about finding the perfect workout routine, or memorizing all the details we covered about BDNF and neurons. If you can just build that habit, your brain will take care of the rest for you.

Final Words

Over the course of this book we've covered tips and strategies for dealing with many of the biggest challenges you'll face as a student, and we've done our best to use research and our own personal experiences to make those tips as useful as we possibly could. But as you dive into your work, you're going to discover other strategies that might be even more effective, or you'll make tweaks that suit your style of working better than anything we could come up with.

And I'd encourage you to actively seek out these improvements, as learning and productivity are two fields where there's no single set of "best" practices. As Bruce Lee once said, "Adapt what is useful, reject what is useless, and add what is specifically your own." And just as Lee himself strove to make this cycle of self-improvement a lifelong process, so should you.

We've covered a lot of ground over the past 10 chapters, but there's always more to learn – both in the realm of study skills and beyond. So keep learning, keep improving, and keep studying.

Printed in Great Britain
by Amazon